REDEMPTIVE PURSUITS

DISCOVER WHAT MATTERS

KENNY KLEPACKI

Copyright © 2025 Kenny Klepacki

All rights reserved. No part of this book may be reproduced, distributed, or transmitted in any form or by any means, including photocopying, recording, or other electronic or mechanical methods, without the prior written permission of the author, except in the case of brief quotations embodied in critical reviews and certain other noncommercial uses permitted by copyright law.

Cover and interior formatting by
KUHN Design Group | kuhndesigngroup.com

To the One who makes every pursuit redemptive

*To my family who taught me that real adventure
begins not on distant roads, but in living
each day with purpose, wonder, and grace*

*And to those brave enough to chase
what truly matters, and humble enough
to be changed by the journey*

CONTENTS

PART I: WHAT AM I PURSUING?

1. Crisis or Adventure 9
2. How did we get here? 15
3. Quiet Rumblings 27
4. Breaking Free 37

PART II: WHERE ARE WE GOING?

5. Recalibrating 53
6. Adjust Your Mirrors 67
7. D-E-C-I-D-E 79

PART III: HOW DO WE FORGE NEW PATHWAYS TOGETHER?

8. Get Going 95
9. Consecrating Time 111
10. The Road to Redemption 127

    About the Author 141

PART I

WHAT AM I PURSUING?

CHAPTER 1

CRISIS OR ADVENTURE

"The only journey is the one within."
RAINER MARIA RILKE

I remember the moment when it was all too much. My wife, Polly, and I stared blankly at the calendar for the upcoming semester. School. Sports. Board meetings. Committee meetings. Church activities. Theater performances.

All good things, right?

So, why was Polly shaking her head and closing her eyes? Her whole body was saying, "No."

It's always a jolt when you come back from traveling and enter the real world again. "Babe, the suitcases are not even unpacked," I tried to be encouraging.

"Just breathe," I continued. "We can do this."

She just kept shaking her head.

She looked at me like, "I don't WANT to do this." Her body language described what was below the surface for all of us. There was a sense of:

Dread.

Fatigue.

Overwhelm.

But how did we get to this point? The calendar is chalk full of activities we chose. Our four children are experiencing a lot of growth. I have been building businesses that are gaining traction, and that comes with responsibility. My wife is the most incredible mom anyone could imagine—staying committed to things that really matter.

But the calendar doesn't lie.

There was no margin.

No time to think.

No time to reflect, enjoy, or take it all in.

When I looked at my wife that day, I could sense the weariness. But without Polly inviting us to slow down, I would have powered through. That has been the attitude of our family for years. Work hard. Play hard. Power though. Do hard things.

We had been sacrificing for two decades, doing just that, and not only were we all exhausted, but there was also a sense that the rhythms we were living weren't working to foster the kind of life we wanted for ourselves and for our children.

When I looked at my wife that day, I knew she was tired. Our oldest was one semester away from college. Having kids young has its benefits. You certainly have more energy. You get to experience the joy of watching them grow while you're still in your prime. You get to enjoy the chaos, the laughter, and the long nights without feeling like they're draining the last bit of you.

After a long day of juggling responsibilities and trying to make everything fit, she finally sighed and said, "Either we are going to go on a midlife adventure, or I am going to have a midlife crisis."

Those words changed our lives.
Crisis or adventure?

How did we get here?

Her words hit me with a force I couldn't ignore—every choice we had made, every path we had followed, all converging in this moment. The next step wasn't just a decision; it was a tipping point, the difference between renewal and regret, the moment that would define everything that came next.

REDEMPTIVE REFLECTION
CHAPTER 1: ADVENTURE OVER CRISIS

This is a moment to listen—to yourself, to your story, to the life that's unfolding around you. You don't have to fix anything right now. Just pay attention. Look gently at your current rhythms. Your calendar. Your choices. Your obligations. Take a deep breath. Find a quiet space. Slow the pace of your mind.

Are there things you're saying yes to that are quietly draining your energy, joy, or presence?

Where do you feel like you're "powering through" rather than living with intention?

Can you name any area of your life that needs to be redeemed?

_____

_____

_____

There is power in naming what's real. And there is freedom in choosing a different way forward. Crisis or adventure?

You get to choose.

CHAPTER 2

HOW DID WE GET HERE?

*"We must let go of the life we have planned,
so as to accept the one that is waiting for us."*
JOSEPH CAMPBELL

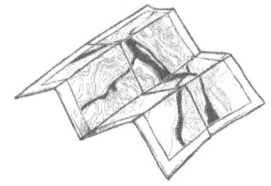

According to my wife, our current system wasn't working. To be honest, I thought we were fine. Better than fine. Her comment that she was on the verge of a midlife crisis caught me off guard. I didn't even know where she was coming from. It's not like we were in the middle of chaos—okay, there was a little bit of chaos—but certainly not at DEFCON Level 1 crisis. We had goals and plans. We took vacations and even traveled internationally. We were not sitting on the couch, watching TV every night. In fact, I would have said that we are already living an adventure.

How did she come to this crossroads? How did we get to this point?

For the next few weeks, I did what I do best—I overthought everything. My mind spun through an endless checklist of what we should be doing. *Did we miss something? What isn't adding up? This doesn't make sense.* The questions looped in my head, each one pulling me deeper into the uncertainty.

Business is growing. Check. The kids are doing well in school and being nourished educationally and spiritually. Check. We are involved at church, volunteering and giving back to the community regularly. Check, check, and check.

On the outside, life was pretty good, at least from a checklist standpoint. We had family and friends and fellowship. We were in good health. On Maslow's hierarchy of needs, the bottom three layers of the pyramid were stacked. This is not the recipe for a crisis.

Or was it?

Is this how it starts? What does she see that I am missing? Instead of getting cranky, I got curious.

Over the next few weeks, this was all Polly and I talked about. Every day we had another micro-conversation that forced us to look under the rug. As she opened up about her frustrations and fears, I gave myself permission to be honest and ask inconvenient questions.

What am I really working toward?

What am I chasing?

What is our family pursuing?

I hit pause and gave myself the space for some much-needed reflection. It was January, but instead of the usual New Year's resolutions, I did something different—I stopped.

Whoa. When was the last time I actually pressed the pause button?

Almost instantly, I felt a new kind of freedom—the kind that comes from simply allowing my mind to slow down. Life was still moving, the train was still on the tracks, but for once, we weren't shoveling coal into the fire.

Can we really afford to slow down? We will lose so much momentum. We should be stepping on the gas harder.

At this point, I was focused on attempting to understand what needed attention before taking any action. I didn't want to make a bad decision. I assumed we would take a couple of weeks, talk about all of this, hire a coach, see a counselor, maybe take a much-needed break and then pick up where we hit the pause button.

One evening, our conversation focused on some possible adventures for the family. We had friends who had recently set off on a sailing adventure.

"I don't want to do the sailing thing," Polly told me, and I agreed. We talked about what 'adventure' looked like for both of us. We thought about extended travel or moving overseas.

But Polly had other ideas.

She already had a vision. Long before I fully grasped it, she knew what she wanted and, more importantly, what our family needed. It wasn't just an idea — it was a feeling, a certainty she carried with her. She had been thinking, planning, and quietly piecing it all together in her mind. Now, she just needed me to catch up.

I was in the middle of a meeting, half-listening to a conversation that suddenly felt far less important, when my phone buzzed. A message from her.

"We are going to the RV show this weekend."

No discussion. No buildup. Just a simple statement of fact. And in that moment, I realized — this wasn't just a casual outing. This was the beginning of something big.

Little did I know, she had already been diving into homeschool curriculums and researching destinations. Soon after that I began receiving a flood of emails with links to RVs, possible routes, and adventures.

My mind was racing. RV travel is just not practical for us! Whatever crisis we are having now will certainly follow us into the RV. We are not going to fix the problem by running or driving away from it. There is no reason to throw away everything we have worked for and set out to do to just walk back into them again.

I didn't know it at the time, but she was not running away from something.

She was running toward something better.

It didn't take much for my curiosity to be piqued. What I experienced were visions of all the places we might see and explore in an RV. Even though it was so different from our current reality, it felt impossible to hold back from dreaming of what a simpler and untethered life might look like for our family.

And maybe that dream had been planted in me long ago. Growing up, some of my best memories were made camping with my family. We weren't extravagant travelers, a cheap pop-up camper and one of my dad's work trucks, but boy did we experience adventure. I remember all the sticks we carved, the campfires, the 'smoke' from our breath on cold nights and mornings. Flat stones that we would skip on lakes and rivers, the fish we caught, the stars. I remember waking up to the sound of birds, zipping up my sleeping bag, and stepping outside the tent into crisp morning air, seeing my parents prep breakfast and drink their coffee. Those trips weren't just vacations — they were freedom for my brother and me. All those memories came rushing back. Maybe I already knew the answers and I just needed a reminder. This opportunity gave me the chance for a break from the routine, a chance to explore, to discover, to be fully present with the people who mattered most in my own life. To go back to my roots and embrace the wonder of childlike adventure.

So off we went, soon finding ourselves walking around the world's largest RV show. I allowed my mind to wander and dream. I gave myself permission to envision us actually doing this.

Could this take our family to a new level of closeness? Could we throw off the bowlines of our life and set off toward something brand new, something no one could define for us?

The thrill of adventure coursed through my veins, urging me to break free from the mundane and dive headfirst into the unknown. Our routine had somehow become a straitjacket. But what if we were to shake things up, repaint the chaos, and rediscover a new rhythm of life?

Embracing the turbulence of a midlife crisis by the prospect of a wild, uncharted adventure opened my mind to something I hadn't felt in a while. The allure of rediscovering passion and purpose in the midst of this demanding phase of life sparked a flame of excitement within me — a feeling that had been buried under years of responsibility, routine, and the quiet sacrifices that come with raising a family. It was more than just a craving for change; it was a deep-seated desire to feel *alive* again, to step beyond the predictable and into the extraordinary.

As we navigated the uncharted waters of this "midlife" season — which, if I was being honest, felt far too early to be called that — visions of a crazy new adventure for our family began to take shape. The more we talked, the more the idea transformed from a reckless impulse into something real, something invigorating. It wasn't about running away from our life but running toward a version of it that was richer, freer, and filled with possibility. With every conversation, with every RV, trailer, camper, and van we looked at, a refreshing perspective began to emerge, painting the unwritten chapters of our future with bold, untamed strokes.

Maybe that's why the idea of an RV adventure didn't feel so foreign. Maybe, deep down, I was being pulled back to something I had always known but somehow forgotten along the way. I had experienced a kind of freedom and connection before as a child but now I longed to create that for my own family.

REDEMPTIVE REFLECTION
CHAPTER 2: WHEN ADVENTURE FINDS YOU

Sometimes change begins not with a decision, but with a whisper. A moment. A conversation that unexpectedly stirs the soul. This reflection is for those moments—when something deep within you begins to ask, "Is this all there is?"

Pause.

Listen.

Reflect.

Often, we move through life by checking off the boxes. Work. Family. Church. Community. All good things—but are they crowding out the deeper questions?

Where in my life might I be settling for comfort over curiosity?

_____

_____

_____

_____

REDEMPTIVE PURSUITS

When was the last time I felt free? Really free?

If I allowed myself to imagine a different kind of life — untethered, adventurous, and deeply connected — what would it look like?

What might I be invited to run toward, not just away from?

The journey toward a more vibrant, meaningful life rarely starts with perfect clarity. It starts with a question. A crack in the plan. A moment of courage. You don't have to see the whole map. You just have to be willing to take the next step.

CHAPTER 3

QUIET RUMBLINGS

"Your life does not get better by chance; it gets better by change."
JIM ROHN

Before the idea of a midlife 'adventure' was a thing for us, I have to admit I was pretty unaware of what was bubbling underneath the surface. Deep down, a storm was brewing, but, honestly, who has time to really deal with that? Life is hard. It is busy and messy. Things stay hidden and suppressed just so we can keep going.

But, as they say, "You don't know what you don't know."

If someone asked how I was doing, I would have confidently asserted that life was going well. I hadn't realized that I was like a vehicle that looks shiny on the outside but upon closer inspection, one discovers previous damage and body filler. The paint may shine but under that illustrious glimmer are problems that will eventually bubble up and reveal corrosion.

The longer you ignore it, the worse it becomes.

We couldn't see the crisis brewing below the surface because we were too comfortable and busy to feel it, let alone pay any attention to it. Have you ever endured a long flight, sitting in the seat for a long time? Your body can become numb. You are simultaneously comfortable and uncomfortable at the same time… until you begin to move. The moment you move, bend, and stretch, you realize how stiff and sore you really are, but you start feeling better. The parts that are numb regain their feeling. After a brief battle of discomfort, you stretch and move again and everything starts feeling better.

Well, like our bodies, our souls, minds, and imaginations are meant to move. We get numb. We sit on things, and our life gets numb to the pain. Sometimes we self-medicate, but often it's a lack of movement over time that causes the numbness.

Our lives need movement. And sometimes redirection.

Newton's law of inertia states an object in motion will stay in motion unless acted upon by an outside force. It's so easy to become unaware of the rumblings of our soul as we sit in our comfortable seats and fly through our busy lives in the same direction.

The good news is that change is possible. As we release the comfort and stretch our legs, we find something better… a deeper calling, a sense of purpose. This is what we are all searching for, deep down. Oftentimes, it takes discomfort and numbness to force us to move.

Somehow, though, in the daily choices of regular life, we find easier ways to get through the day. This ease and busyness of modern life appear better but these counterfeits never last. They cannot replace purpose, meaning, peace, and contentment.

Comfort masks our problems, and our busyness can distract us from the thing we really want. Things we really need.

Of course, it's not just comfort that masks the storm brewing inside us. John Mark Comer writes, "The modern world is a virtual conspiracy against the inner life." Everything in our over-scheduled, technology-focused, commercialized world drowns out a rich inner life.

At the time, I didn't want to hear my wife confronting me with the truth about what she was experiencing below the surface because I would have to deal with my own rumblings and discomfort. This culminating moment was the "outside force" our family needed to course correct.

I knew that I had become too focused on comfort and self-preservation. We are all wired to do just that! Particularly within family life, it is easy to focus too much on providing safety, security, and routines that ensure our loved ones are taken care of.

Do we ever stop to think about what our children are losing as we focus so much on keeping life safe and predictable? Do we really understand what's going on beneath the surface—how they might be struggling in ways we don't see, how their spirit might be growing weaker as they face fewer challenges?

There is freedom from pain, struggle and discomfort. But in trying to remove all hardships, we forget that real freedom isn't just about avoiding difficulties—it's about having freedom for growth, discovery, learning, and becoming stronger through life's ups and downs. By protecting our children from every struggle, we might also be keeping them from the very experiences that help them grow, build resilience, and find their true strength. So, what is it we are really seeking? Freedom *from* or freedom *for*?

John Eldridge, author of *Wild at Heart*, writes, "Deep in his heart, every man longs for a battle to fight, an adventure to live, and a beauty to rescue." This quote resonated with me now more than ever. We are seeking freedom for a meaningful fight, an adventure, and a rescue.

At the time, our oldest daughter, Madi, was eighteen years old. She was just beginning her quest of searching for identity, belonging, purpose, navigating the expected existential crisis of launching into adulthood. This new season of life created a natural catalyst for change. Our emotions were high, and it felt like everything in our family was shifting as she took this big step.

Our next oldest daughter, Reese, was 11 at the time, nearing her teenage years and would undoubtedly be asking "Who am I?" in various ways. She was entering middle school, a time of discovery and challenges, and we wanted to give her an environment in which to grow into all that she could be—a sanctuary where her curiosity could flourish, her confidence could be nurtured, and her dreams could take flight without fear or limitation.

This was more than just about academics; it was about fostering her musical talent, encouraging her individuality, independence as well as interdependence, and ensuring she knew that no matter what the world threw at her, she had a solid foundation of love, support, grit and gratitude to stand on.

Our son, Wes, was seven years old, full of life, energy, and already loved exploring and adventure. His boundless curiosity led him to see the world as an endless playground, where every day held the promise of new discoveries. We wanted to nurture that spark in him, to give him the freedom to learn and grow in new and exciting environments.

The youngest of the bunch, Corinne, was only three years old so every day was a new day of discovery and wide-eyed adventure. She needed the freedom to wonder.

Every one of our children was in their own season of change. We had no idea we were about to embark on a redemptive journey—a quest to better understand ourselves and one another, striving for a more authentic life both individually and as a family. We didn't know what form this change would take, but we knew something was off, and we couldn't afford to ignore it any longer.

It became crystal clear this is the road we were going to travel. And so, the day we got home from the RV show, we just started. No one showed us the way; we had no road map, no agenda, no knowledge about this way of life. We just jumped right in, spending the next few months learning everything we could about what unit to buy, how to operate, maintain, live and enjoy it.

After our research was complete, we eventually bought an RV and spent the next few months trip planning, reading, researching, and talking with folks who had done it before. We had no idea what was ahead, but we tried to be as prepared as possible, hopeful for real change and powerful movement in our lives. We were equipped with some really fun tools and ready to make what seemed impossible, finally possible.

So off we went.

REDEMPTIVE REFLECTION
CHAPTER 3: DO YOU HEAR THAT?

Change rarely begins with clarity. It begins with a quiet rumbling—a tension beneath the surface that asks us to pay attention.

Do you sense a stirring that you want to name today? When you are quiet and honest, what are you sensing?

Where have I grown numb without realizing it?

Am I seeking freedom from *something... or freedom* for *something greater?*

What would it look like to pursue a life of adventure, discovery, and purpose instead of just avoiding risk or discomfort?

The invitation isn't just to change your life. It's to awaken it. You have permission to pay attention to what's stirring beneath the surface and trust that even in the discomfort, there is purpose, movement, and the possibility of something better.

CHAPTER 4

BREAKING FREE

*"Two roads diverged in a wood, and I—
I took the one less traveled by,
And that has made all the difference."*

ROBERT FROST

Spending three years visiting 30+ states, countless cities, and over 100+ national parks and historic sites teaches you a lot. Not to mention all the countless state parks and recreational areas, breweries, wineries, bakeries, restaurants, children's museums, off the wall quirky places, Walmarts, thrift stores, friends' front yards and driveways, riverbanks, botanical gardens, marinas, forests, beaches, deserts, mountains and valleys.

And then there are the people you meet along the way.

The one thing that didn't really change was the necessity to continue to work and complete school assignments from the road. It certainly looked different but the perspective on life was completely reoriented. It was an adventure that reframed our lives and changed the trajectory of our family. It was such a dramatic shift in our perspective that we all decided together to return to our family home in St. Petersburg, Florida. The conclusion of our RV journey wasn't a final farewell-it was the catalyst that transformed our outlook and emboldened us to embrace a new chapter of epic adventures.

We had no idea that God would use our trip to redeem our hearts and our time in the most thrilling way I could imagine through the unforgettable moments of sheer terror, beauty, wonder, awe, and amazement. And that was just looking at the kids!

Who knew that there could be such an incredible way to know my wife and my children better, understand the longings of their hearts, and relate to them on a whole new level?

I can remember so many evenings after a wild and adventurous day of exploring, hiking, sightseeing, exploring that we would find ourselves around a campfire, bellies full from a simple but perfect meal, reflecting on the day and the challenges that we faced, the scenery we stared at, or the wildlife and the people we encountered but more often than not, it was the lessons that we learned through the shared experiences Most days were fairly exhausting but fulfilling. The kids usually started the day full of energy, racing ahead on the trail, but they would often hit a wall somewhere along the way. The enthusiasm would fade, and their laughter would often turn into complaints. "Why do we have to do this?" "Can't we just go back to the RV?" "I'm tired."

And often, I would feel the same. But something in me knew that if we pushed through, we'd find what we came for. And we did. We would see it in each other.

The grumblings would almost always turn into "Wow." "We did it." "I can't believe we made it." "What a view!" "Let's do it again!"

The kids would relive and unpack all those adventure moments from their own perspectives around the dinner table or around a campfire. I would watch them laugh about slipping in the mud, reenacting a ridiculous encounter with an overly curious squirrel, and replaying their moment of triumph at the top. We didn't have Wi-Fi. There was often no cell service. But there was something better — an unhurried space to reflect, to talk, to just be together.

We did it. We finally found "it."

After returning to solid ground and taking time to meditate on the effects of this great adventure, I cannot imagine what our lives would look like now without this experience during such a critical time in our family. It was so transformative that it has become my life's mission to give people similar transformational experiences as they are making decisions about what is most important. I am forever grateful for the time my family got to redeem in our rolling apartment. Here's the thing, you don't need an extreme adventure. Just a little coaching and guidance, strategic planning, clarity of vision, mission and personal values. Anyone can gain clarity, connect with loved ones, and move closer to their highest impact in life with a different perspective.

People frequently ask our family, "What did you learn?" or "What were the biggest takeaways from your grand adventure?" In the following chapters, I'll do my best to put our answers into words. But more than that, I hope that as you read, you'll experience a shift in your own perspective—a vision of life that feels bigger, bolder, and more epic than what you've known until now. I truly believe that embracing this shift is key to personal growth, achieving life goals, and nurturing family relationships, no matter where they currently stand.

FREEDOM OF TIME

The first lesson from our journey of "reperspectifying" our life is simple yet profound: we just needed more time together to create those transformative moments. Breakthroughs don't happen on a schedule — they emerge from the sheer abundance of time shared. As the saying goes, "Quality time doesn't exist without quantity time." The more hours we invested, the richer the experiences and the deeper the connections became.

Shift your mindset from "I want quality time" to "I'll give more quantity of time to myself and my loved ones," and the quality will follow naturally. Time is our most valuable asset and how we redeem it shapes the richness of our lives and relationships. The truth is that any time that you dedicate becomes meaningful when you're fully present. Spend that time in extraordinary places, creating inviting spaces, culminating in unforgettable moments through incredible, shared experiences.

It's about doing — making the conscious decision to invest your time in ways that enrich your life and the lives of those around you.

When it comes to relationships, especially with children, the importance of time becomes even more apparent. We often hear that we have only 18 summers with our kids, a limited window to make a lasting impact. But an even more sobering way to look at it is a child has 18 summers as a child with about 12 or 13 of those that they will actually remember.

It's easy to get caught up in the daily grind and postpone meaningful experiences, thinking that there will always be more time. But the truth is, time is fleeting. As one dad lamented to me, "My son is a sophomore in high school, and we haven't done anything meaningful." This realization can be a wake-up call to prioritize those moments before they slip away but the truth is, it's never too late.

The concept of "redeeming time" is not just about spending time but about making that time as impactful and intentional as possible. Get away. Invest in being with those you truly care about and those who want you to win at life. Invest time meditating, thinking, pondering, quietly listening for the Creator, waiting to hear that still, small voice.

Whether it's creating memories that your family will carry with them for the rest of their lives, providing experiences that transform them, or doing things that invite them back into the story of your life, the time you invest is never wasted and will always matter.

Even if you've missed opportunities in the past, it's never too late to start making a difference. The moment you realize the importance of time is the moment you can begin to make it count.

More is more.
Take more time.

Carve it out every week, every month, and every year.

REDEEMING THE TIME

Redeeming time involves using each moment purposefully, a concept rooted in Ephesians 5:16: "Redeeming the time, because the days are evil." This principle emphasizes seizing opportunities, avoiding wasted effort, and living with moral clarity, especially during challenging times.

In our modern, fast-paced world, practicing mindful living becomes essential. By making deliberate choices that reflect our core values and long-term goals, we can navigate daily life more effectively. This mindfulness allows us to recognize and seize subtle opportunities for growth and connection, such as pursuing new learning experiences, strengthening relationships, or embracing unexpected adventures.

Efficient stewardship ties these concepts together by encouraging us to manage our time wisely—organizing our days, eliminating inefficiencies, and prioritizing what truly matters.

Aligning our schedules with our goals and values ensures that our energy is directed toward actions that foster personal growth and meaningful living.

In essence, redeeming time is not about doing more but about focusing on what matters most. By embracing mindful living, seizing opportunities, valuing each moment, and practicing efficient stewardship, we can create a life where every day contributes to a lasting legacy of growth and fulfillment.

STEP BACK AND PUSH BACK

Reclaiming your time, and beginning your journey toward a more meaningful life, means letting go of the activities that drain you. This will require you to make hard choices and take an honest look at your aspirations, abilities, and core values to determine what truly matters.

My wife instinctively knew that this adventure wasn't just something we wanted, it was something we desperately needed. Deep down, we both felt we were unintentionally shortchanging our kids, trading what truly mattered for the demands of the moment or worse, doing it because that is what we thought we were supposed to do. But breaking free from the pull of everyday expectations and having the courage to say, "No" to the usual routines, even for a week or a month, was a bold move. It's not easy, but sometimes the most meaningful choices require stepping away from the ordinary, the traditional, the comfortable, and stepping into the wild, dangerous, and unknown.

Imagine choosing to set aside all the typical Thanksgiving or Christmas traditions and focusing solely on what genuinely brings your family joy and renewal. Making that choice means stepping back from the familiar and resisting the weight of others' expectations. It takes courage to carve out your own path, to pursue the vision you have and want, to prioritize what truly enriches your loved ones. But by doing so, you reclaim the holidays as a time for meaningful connection and authentic experiences, creating memories that resonate far beyond the season.

If you choose to step back and take your children out of the traditional five-days-a-week school system to create more space for personal growth, rest, and meaningful family time, you might face societal, family, or peer pressure. Yet, when you have confidence in your decisions and an alignment to your values, the courage to hold your ground becomes priceless. It changes you. True fulfillment often lies in daring to prioritize what truly matters, even when it goes against the grain.

Clarifying your vision for your family helps you define the mission, the things you need to do, in order to see your vision become reality. By making a plan and making your personal reflection a priority, you create a roadmap for turning your dreams into tangible outcomes. This intentional focus ensures that your time, energy, and actions align with what matters most, empowering you and your family to thrive in ways that truly resonate with your values and aspirations.

For us, stepping back meant finding stillness through quiet prayer and truly listening for God's voice above all others. We had an idea of what we wanted, but it wasn't until we stepped away from the noise of daily life and tuned in that we could clearly hear. And the further we went into the unknown, the more we depended on His voice and leading and the more evident it became that we were where we were supposed to be.

It also meant fighting for our kids' freedom. We had to fight against year-round sports, musical recitals, and the race to valedictorian that begins in kindergarten.

Whatever you are pushing back against, trust your instincts. If there is a voice encouraging you to rest on Sunday, do it.

If you know that you need to unplug and get back to nature, find a park close to you and skip those events that you must attend.

If you know you need time to think then take it. If you need to breathe fresh air, I have good news. It is still there. It's just outside your door. Close the book that someone else told you was important to read or the spreadsheet and just dare to be.

As you close this chapter, ask yourself: What if every day could be an opportunity to reclaim the moments that truly matter? Imagine shedding the distractions that steal your time and daring to invest in deep, transformative experiences, whether through heartfelt conversations with loved ones or stepping into the unknown with bold determination. This journey challenges you to look beyond routine and to create a life rich with intentional connections and memorable adventures. Embrace the possibility that by choosing what to honor with your time, you can reshape your entire world.

REDEMPTIVE REFLECTION
CHAPTER 4: BREAKING FREE

Sometimes we must step away from what's familiar to rediscover what truly matters. This reflection is about breaking free; from routine, from pressure, from the lies that tell us there's only one way to live well. Let these questions guide your soul toward more space, more intention, and more meaningful connection. Think honestly about how your time is currently spent.

Where in my life do I need to take back time — and how might I use that time more intentionally?

_____

_____

_____

_____

What am I really fighting for?

_____

_____

_____

_____

When I think about my family, my future, my faith — what is worth protecting?

What would 'breaking free' look like for me or my family — and what bold move might help us get there?

You don't need to wait for the perfect time. You don't need to have all the answers.

You just need to take one courageous step toward what matters most—and trust that the freedom you're seeking is found on the road less traveled.

PART II

WHERE ARE WE GOING?

CHAPTER 5

RECALIBRATING

"A change of place plus a change of pace equals a change of perspective."
MARK BATTERSON

Adventure and exploration have always been part of my life. When I was growing up, my parents were pretty adventurous and took my brother and me on some fun, memorable travel experiences. We called them vacations, but they were planned adventures.

As an adult, a man, a father and a husband, every new 'place' seemed to have lost its excitement. The pace at which we lived life was exceedingly challenging to keep up with. The moments seemed to slip by, and the familiarity of places dulled the desire for adventure. Age and a little bit of success created too much need and want for comfort.

But the RV trip changed everything. It brought that childlike adventure back into my life. This book was not written to convince you to buy an RV and escape your busy life. In fact, it's just the opposite.

I don't want you to follow me.

I certainly don't want you to escape your life.

I want you to discover a more authentic life for yourself and those you love and care for.

I have found that there are certain underlying principles that, when present, can turn any life pursuit into a redemptive one. It has become my mission to help individuals, families, and organizations use these principles as a framework for redeeming broken threads in ourselves, with God, and with others.

NOT JUST A VACATION – MORE THAN AN ESCAPE

The adventures in this book go far beyond mere escapes—they aren't just vacations, getaways, or retreats. While people take trips all the time, most never cross into the realm of true redemption. On a typical vacation, you might explore new sights, taste new foods, visit unfamiliar places, relax, and create memories to savor life a little more. But rarely do people use the shift in scenery as an opportunity to gain deeper insight into their life, goals, and relationships. These adventures are about transforming how you see the world—and yourself.

Redemptive recreation is more intentional, and the effects are often life changing. On vacation, a change in perspective is short-lived and accidental. Vacationers stumble upon new ideas and those ideas disappear out of their minds as quickly as they enter with only the feelings of enrichment to be short-lived and a few photos to memorialize their experiences. The goal of vacation is to provide a temporary escape, and therefore, vacationers return to their lives and return to the same old problems without any new perspectives.

So, the first step in planning a redemptive voyage is a shift in mindset. When you plan a redemptive trip, you are planning it with the goal of gaining a different perspective and then giving yourself permission to let that new perspective fuel your everyday life. When you leave, you are leaving your old self behind and forging a new, unknown trail.

In the movie, "What Happens Later," Meg Ryan asks her old friend, "Are you on a trip or a journey?" In order to go on a trip, you simply hop on a plane or load the car. In order to go on a journey, a person also commits to a shift in mindset. He or she is open to the idea that this experience could change their lives forever. It involves an openness to change that influences the rest of daily life.

On a trip, you momentarily change your location.

On a journey, you forever change your perspective.

CHANGE OF PLACE

For true redemptive recreation, a change of place is essential. As Mark Batterson puts it, "A change of place plus a change of pace equals a change in perspective." The key ingredient is the new environment. A fresh setting signals to our brains that something different is unfolding. It prompts us to wake up and pay attention. The unfamiliarity of a new place—the unknown streets, the hidden gems waiting to be discovered—ignites a sense of adventure and awakens our curiosity to explore, learn, and uncover what we didn't expect. It's why the travel and tourism industry is an $11 trillion dollar global sector—responsible for an estimated 1 in 8 jobs around the world.

Our brains are absolutely incredible organs! They help us survive, partly by ignoring much of our surroundings. Our brains are hard wired to ignore 90% of what we see on a regular basis. How could I possibly even drive to work if I noticed every blade of grass on my way to the office? Oftentimes, when we are in new places, we can find ourselves out of place. This is why visitors to your city see so much more than you do. You are in survival mode in your city. You are working hard, getting kids to school on time, finishing projects for work, folding the laundry, and pumping gas.

But have you ever hosted a friend or relative in your hometown? I am always surprised by the wonder and amazement people discover when they visit us in our hometown. They take tours of museums that I pass by every day. They relish architectural features of buildings that I regularly ignore. They savor food that I take for granted. Why? They are outside their regular routine! They are experiencing the benefit of new surroundings.

So, traveling to a new location, even if it's just a new garden that you have never visited, gives you a clear advantage. It provides a level of openness that just does not exist in your regular surroundings. In your hometown, you are like a train on an invisible railroad. The train of your life is set and running regularly with predictable speed and stops. You are working on your laptop while the train races by, and even if all the answers to life exist in your hometown, you cannot see them from inside the train.

To go on a redemptive journey, you must intentionally derail internally/mentally.

Cut the line.

Detached from the routine.

Not only are you more alive and more aware of your surroundings in a new place, but you are also free from the molds and boundaries that others are often placing on you. I specifically recall the freedom the campgrounds afforded my children.

When we pulled up to a new campground, no one knew us. Therefore, we could be whoever we wanted to be. I could say, "My name is Sam," or "People call me George," and that was fine other than it wasn't truthful. But it was so freeing to be just me. My children could break free from stereotypes they were forced into at school. They could shake off any family molds that had been placed on them.

We are all unconsciously putting ourselves into molds that society has created for us. How many movies have we seen when a teenager breaks out of his or her defined mold of a jock, princess, or nerd? It makes for fun television drama because it's hard to do! By traveling to a new location, it's easier. The new place is like a red carpet, inviting us to walk down a new path for ourselves. That path is wide open. No one is stopping us with their preconceived notions of how we should act.

Each time our family went somewhere new, we became a little bit different. We became a little bit more authentic. This is part of the edge that a redemptive adventure provides. You give yourself a shortcut to discovering the real YOU. I think our family could have made this discovery in about ten years, after a lot of counseling, but the change of place allowed us to expedite these revelations.

CHANGE OF PACE

If we traveled all over the world, but returned back to the regular To Do List, this whole experiment would break down. In order to gain perspective, it's critical to change the pace at which you are operating and really create margin, not just in our minds, but in our calendars.

For our family, we ventured into the RV life. You can only go so fast and so far in an RV. The mere driving dynamics forced us to change our pace. It forced us to have to drive through places we had chosen to fly over before.

By taking more time "off" than the normal 2-4 weeks, the pace of our calendar slowed as well.

Pace is defined as a "consistent and continuous speed in walking, running, or moving." Pace is calculated by distance and time to give us a measurement of how fast and far we are going. During our normal routine, we were moving at an unbelievable pace.

In the past, our pace was consistently fast. Everyone in the family was running off to activities while the parents were the air traffic controllers.

The goals and dreams we were working towards in our life were big. There is nothing wrong with big lofty dreams and goals. But we wanted to achieve them as fast as we possibly could. We were racing at breakneck speed towards the horizon. The pace at which we were operating our life and living out the schedules in our calendar was an indicator of the pace we were operating at in our minds. At 34,000 feet above the ground traveling at 500 mph, you don't pay much attention to the little towns or cities, the forests or the rivers below.

But when you drive the same path on the ground at 45 mph through the small towns and over the bridges that cross the same rivers, it allows you to actually take in the beauty of what you are seeing and experiencing. Same direction. Same destination. Slower pace.

It's the same in life. American life has become so busy. We are like airplanes, flying over our lives at such an outrageous pace, never allowing ourselves the time to process what we are experiencing, missing the beauty, awe, and wonder of most of it.

If time is one of our most precious commodities, why do we put more effort into gaining more of it back?

By slowing down, taking the scenic route, we allow ourselves the opportunity to do some deep critical thinking and soul searching. While you can see a river or a mountain range from an airplane, you really can't process the sheer beauty of sitting beside it or climbing to the top of it. We can even make connections and draw conclusions. None of that could happen at the pace of a typical American family's life.

Traveling at a slower pace creates the space to appreciate the 'in-betweens'—those moments when you can hear the music, absorb the surroundings, or simply reflect in silence. Redemption, like change, takes time. It requires moments of stillness to think, synthesize, and draw deeper conclusions. By slowing down, you give yourself the gift of being able to process and truly experience transformation.

Let me ask you a few questions. When was the last time the pace of your life slowed down? Has it ever slowed down? How did it make you feel?

Approach this journey with the mindset that something new is about to be revealed to you. Prepare yourself to change both your place and your pace, knowing that the ultimate goal is to gain a fresh perspective on how you see the world. By embracing this shift, you open yourself to the transformative experiences that lie ahead, allowing new insights to shape the way you live and engage with those around you.

REDEMPTIVE REFLECTION
CHAPTER 5: RECALIBRATING

Sometimes, we need to leave the familiar to see clearly again. This reflection is about the power of recalibrating through a change of place and pace—and how these shifts can lead us into deeper clarity, freedom, and transformation.

What is the pace of my life telling me?

Am I moving so fast that I'm missing what matters most? Explain.

Is there a location, setting, or environment I've been drawn to?

What molds are preventing me from growth in my current location?

Change of place. Change of pace. Change of perspective. You don't need an RV or a long sabbatical. You just need the willingness to step off the path for a while—and pay attention.

Let this be your invitation to recalibrate, to wonder, and to rediscover what really matters.

CHAPTER 6

ADJUST YOUR MIRRORS

"The greater the stillness the clearer the reflection."
UNKNOWN

With the change in pace and surroundings, you will likely begin to experience a sense of renewal. As you release your usual schedule, you can release your usual thoughts. This is where breakthroughs become possible.

You are now genuinely redeeming your time. Your mind is likely liberated by a new perspective. Now is the perfect time to ask questions. This is the space to ask yourself those big questions. You know the ones — the questions you don't have time for in the middle of the usual race.

At home, I have some amazing advisors who help me make strategic decisions. I have service providers like my accountant and financial advisor who makes sure that I get the most out of an asset or property. I meet with them regularly and they ask me questions about my goals and based on those answers; they formulate a plan.

But a tax advisor cannot give me answers about my most important resource—my time.

For that, I have to ask myself a different set of questions and find a different guide.

Are you deploying the asset of your time in the most purposeful way possible? If you don't spend the time to really be honest with yourself about the rhythm of your life, your core values, or the mission and vision you have for your life, you will never truly experience them.

The goal of the following questions is to connect to your soul. Now that you are finally open enough and free enough to think beyond your usual routine, it's time to truly ponder.

Take a few hours, a few days, or a few weeks to journal through these questions. As you hike or explore, bring these questions with you. It's okay to answer one question in ten different ways.

Do not rush.

These are not questions designed for fast response. They are prompts to lead you into deeper exploration of yourself. As you answer these questions, you are buying yourself some space. You are creating a new rhythm. Your brain is reconnecting memories and creating pathways for you to make new ones. You are intentionally slowing the train and giving yourself permission to pull into the station for a while. You are releasing all the pressure valves and letting go of the ego in order to find your authentic self.

As you answer each question, and experience the beauty of a new place, you are experiencing yourself in a new way and thus knowing yourself in a new way.

Embrace the moments of quiet during the questions.

Lean into the blank space.

You are not escaping anything; you are finding the truest version of yourself. Notice where you wrestle with yourself. Allow time to go to the deepest place in your soul.

LOOKING BACK

1. What childhood memories make you truly happy?

___

___

___

___

2. Can you recall a moment when you felt a deep sense of fulfillment? What were you doing?

___

___

___

___

3. What past successes have been meaningful to you?

___

___

___

___

4. When was a time you felt genuinely at peace? What were the circumstances?

5. What were some turning points in your life that led you to focus on more meaningful activities?

6. How do your memories of joy influence the way you seek happiness today?

7. What memories bring you a sense of pride?

---

8. Describe a specific memory of kindness (either given or received) that stands out to you.

---

9. How do your memories of achievement or recognition influence your pursuit of goals today?

---

10. What past experiences have reinforced the importance of aligning your time with your values?

LOOKING INWARD

11. What are you feeling right now?

12. How would you describe your inner life in the past year? 5 years? 10 years?

13. Are there any feelings or ponderings you regularly ignore?

14. What is bringing you energy and hope on a regular basis?

15. What part of your life do you want to build on?

LOOKING AHEAD

16. If one year from now, you are sitting in this same place and reflecting on the fact that this was the most joy-filled and successful year of your life, what happened?

---

17. If you could make one decision that would forever change the trajectory of your life, what would it be?

---

18. If you used your unique perspective, past, abilities, and struggles to do the thing that only you could do, what would that be?

---

19. What does authenticity feel like to you?

20. How could you take one step to living a more authentic and connected life?

CHAPTER 7

D-E-C-I-D-E

"Decisions determine destiny."
TONY ROBBINS

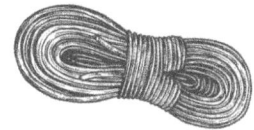

After taking the time for deep reflection, you will most likely discover that there is a need for change. You have gotten much-needed perspective so let's make the most of it! It's time to D-E-C-I-D-E.

As a pilot, I appreciate the idea that there are only two types of people on an aircraft—pilots and passengers. The pilots are making critical decisions to guide the plane to its destination while passengers only have to decide between what to eat and drink or what movie to watch.

If you have ever traveled on a plane before, you have most likely not been in the cockpit, especially while airborne. I am inviting you into the pilot's seat (the left seat) to take control of your life. The process in this chapter is based on principles that save your life while flying. We call it A.D.M., Aeronautical Decision Making, because pilots must be expert decision makers. A pilot is constantly monitoring and analyzing everything around them. They have studied charts, maps, and procedures. They know their aircraft, what temperature and pressure the oil needs to be, how much fuel is on board, and how much longer they have to go. An entire flight is simply one good decision after another until we arrive safely on the runway.

Becoming a good decision-maker and having critical thinking skills is essential to creating the life you want and simply making one good decision after another. Just like a pilot, you have some constants in your life, but you also are dealing with a barrage of variables and new information as you make decisions for your family, business, finances, and community every day. This process will help you make rapid decisions and act with confidence that you are moving toward the right decision and destination.

D – DETERMINE THAT A CHANGE IS NEEDED

The first step in the process is "Determine" that change is needed. This realization can come from internal feelings or external pressures or from checklists, accountability or from personal assessments. Sometimes, it's a subtle internal whisper telling you something isn't right; other times, external circumstances or people close to you alert that things aren't going as they should. Regardless of the source, this moment marks the beginning of your journey toward transformation. It's that point of recognition when you admit that staying on the same path is no longer sustainable.

When Polly told me that she was going to have a "midlife crisis or a midlife adventure," I determined very quickly that something needed to change. My internal alarms were going off. I had to methodically separate the emotional from the equation and pull out the critical thinking skills. The moment you determine that a shift is necessary is a powerful one—but it is not where the answers lie. The decision to change isn't the solution itself but rather the crucial first step. If you already had the answers, you'd likely be achieving the results you desire. Instead, deciding to change opens the door to possibility, requiring you to step into the unknown.

This moment of decision is often filled with tension between fear and faith. Fear tells you to cling to the familiar, while faith invites you to see what you believe in the possibility of something better. Both require belief—but where will you put yours? Deciding to move forward means choosing faith over fear, acknowledging that although you don't yet have all the answers, you are ready to pursue them.

E – ESTIMATE THE COST

The second phase in the process, "Estimate," focuses on evaluating what it will take to make the change you've decided is necessary. This process involves considering the resources, sacrifices, and potential outcomes associated with your decision.

Change always comes with a cost, whether it's tangible or intangible. It might require creating hard boundaries in relationships, shifting priorities, or investing more time and effort into areas you've neglected. If you're not seeing the results you want, or if essential parts of your life aren't where they need to be, you may need to go back and build those foundations.

Estimating involves asking yourself tough questions: What do I need to give up to get where I want to go? What's the cost of not making this change? Remember, the cost of doing nothing has consequences as well. You might realize that avoiding change comes at the expense of missed opportunities and deeper fulfillment. However, understanding the costs isn't just about what you'll lose. It's also about recognizing the hidden, unseen costs — those sacrifices you may not immediately anticipate but are inevitable on the road to transformation.

As a pilot, you must estimate the fuel, distance and time needed to make sure you make it to wherever you need to go. Similarly, in life, you must gauge what you deem important or essential for your adventure, whether you have the necessary resources—time, energy, and commitment—to reach your desired outcome.

C – CRAFT A DESIRABLE OUTCOME

You need to change, and you've counted the cost. Now, it's time to have a vision for what you want to build. Hellen Keller said, "The only thing worse than having no sight is having sight with no vision."

You cannot execute upon that which you cannot imagine. If you can draw it, you can build it. Brick by brick and layer by layer, you can make anything a reality, but you must first be bold enough to imagine it and then draw it out or record it.

At this stage, do not worry about how. Design a clear WHAT in this phase.

What are you changing?

What are you creating?

What can you envision for your life?

What does your destination look like?

Crafting a vision for your future, or the future of your organization, means daring to dream big, often beyond what seems immediately possible. It demands that you break free from the limitations of your current reality and imagine a different one—one that aligns with your highest ambitions and values.

This act of visioning isn't for the faint of heart, as it requires both vulnerability and strength, the ability to embrace uncertainty while steadfastly believing in the power of your aspirations.

I – IDENTIFY THE WHO AND THE HOW

When gathering the necessary things that will begin to reshape your life, get into the habit of asking who, not how. Who are the people in your life who can save you time and effort with their expertise? These are your advisors, coaches, accountants, attorneys, and consultants—individuals who help you avoid reinventing the wheel.

Beyond the professionals, consider those who have successfully built something similar to your vision. They are trailblazers who can offer insight into the process, sharing valuable lessons and strategies. These mentors or models of success are critical in helping you avoid pitfalls and accelerate progress.

Tony Robbins famously tells us to, "Model the masters" as a shortcut to everything in life.

Ask yourself:

- Who has already brought a vision like yours to life?
- Who could point you in the right direction?
- Who has written a book on the subject?
- Who is sharing advice on social media, blogs, or online articles?

The answers to those questions will lead you down a much different path than sitting in front of a blank computer screen or notebook as you fumble your way through the idea.

The "hows" relate to the methods and strategies for gathering your team and executing the plan. Rather than relying on casual connections like neighbors for such an important task, it's essential to seek out experienced professionals and people who align with your vision.

Learn from those who have walked the path before you, studying their approach to achieve similar results.

D – DO IT.

Doing something means moving from thought to tangible steps. This is massive. You are taking massive action with massive consequences. You know you need a change. You have counted the cost and crafted a compelling vision. Once you figure out who will help you and how it will get done, it's time to make it happen.

This is where the rubber meets the road—when ideas stop being abstract and start becoming reality. The first step is crucial, and while it may seem daunting, it's actually easier than you might expect. You've already built momentum in your mind; now it's about aligning your actions with the mental game plan you've created.

The key is to take that first step with intention.

Once you're in motion, it's easier to maintain momentum. By the time you've reached this stage, you've already overcome the biggest barrier—inaction. Now, it's about keeping that energy flowing and continuously pushing forward. With each action, you get closer to your goal, and the more you do, the more natural it becomes to take even bigger steps.

E – EXECUTE, EVALUATE AND ENJOY
THE EFFECTS OF YOUR MASSIVE ACTION TAKING.

The final step in the process, "Execute, Evaluate and Enjoy," is about executing the plan and the work to completion. Once completed, reflect on how far you've come and appreciate the fruits of your labor. Often, we don't realize the progress we've made until we measure backwards, comparing where we are now to where we started. This retrospective gives us the ability to see what we're truly capable of, often surprising ourselves with how much we've accomplished.

The plan comes first because knowing where you want to go gives purpose to every step you take. Measuring progress day by day helps you stay on track, but it's crucial not to get lost in the data. Instead, see these metrics as markers of your journey, not the final goal.

At the end of the process, take time to enjoy what you've achieved. You're not just chasing a return on your investment of time and effort; you're running for the reward of accomplishing something meaningful. Reflect on the distance you've traveled and allow yourself to enjoy the results of your hard work.

Evaluating your progress is not just about numbers but about recognizing the transformation and savoring the success you've earned.

REDEMPTIVE REFLECTION
CHAPTER 7: TAKE FLIGHT

Big decisions shape the story of our lives. But the most powerful choices often begin with clarity and commitment. This reflection walks you through a process inspired by how pilots make decisions—with purpose, perspective, and precision. Use these prompts to chart your next bold step.

D—DETERMINE THAT A CHANGE IS NEEDED
Where in my life do I feel a pull for change?

_____

_____

_____

_____

E—ESTIMATE THE COST
What will this change require of me—time, energy, boundaries, money?

_____

_____

_____

_____

Am I willing to pay the price for the future I want?

C—CRAFT A DESIRABLE OUTCOME

What does success look like for me?

What's the clearest picture I can imagine of where this decision could take me?

I—IDENTIFY THE WHO'S AND HOW'S

Who has done something like this before — and what can I learn from them?

―――――――――――――――――――――――――――

―――――――――――――――――――――――――――

―――――――――――――――――――――――――――

―――――――――――――――――――――――――――

D—DO IT.

What's one bold step I can take this week to move forward?

―――――――――――――――――――――――――――

―――――――――――――――――――――――――――

―――――――――――――――――――――――――――

―――――――――――――――――――――――――――

E—EXECUTE, EVALUATE, AND ENJOY

What does it mean to enjoy the journey — not just the destination?

―――――――――――――――――――――――――――

―――――――――――――――――――――――――――

―――――――――――――――――――――――――――

How can I create space to savor the wins and recognize how far I've come?

Your next breakthrough doesn't come from knowing everything—it comes from making the next right decision. Clarity. Courage. Commitment. DECIDE.

PART III

HOW DO WE FORGE NEW PATHWAYS TOGETHER?

CHAPTER 8

GET GOING

"To travel is to take a journey into yourself."
DANNY KAYE

It can be easy to think about your travels as just another vacation or getaway, but your "trip" is so much more than an escape. It's an opportunity for you to have a redemptive experience where renewal and lasting change can be found.

Planning for redemptive recreation is different. It requires a higher level of intentionality but doesn't necessarily require more work. Oftentimes, it requires less!

When Polly and I decided to take a detour, we couldn't share our intentions because we didn't know how to articulate what we were after. We knew we needed and wanted a trajectory change but couldn't figure out how to plan or execute on that goal or who could get us there. When we would map a route for the next leg of the trip, we became better at it simply by committing to it. We developed language for talking about what we wanted based on the experiences we were having and as we traveled through the United States. Our planning became more intentional through trial and error, adjusting to the feedback we were getting from the kids and what we felt in our gut and learning from our own experiences.

Eventually, it became so natural to share what we learned from our experiences. It's one of the main reasons for writing this book. It is my attempt to put into words how others could do something similar. Even if you're not setting off for the open road or braving the open oceans, you can implement these principles and strategies to unlock the secrets of turning pursuits into redemptive experiences.

My heartbeat is to help individuals, families, and organizations find their redemptive story through incredible experiences, ones that are conducive to true life-change. Over the years, I've put my process to the test—learning from every misstep, refining my approach, and witnessing its success firsthand. Today, I'm proud to share this trusted roadmap with you, one that has guided me through transformative journeys and can help you thoughtfully plan your own life-changing adventure.

At the heart of this process are the 5 P's: People, Place, Program, Purpose, and Pursuit. You can start with any of the key elements and begin weaving them together to create the framework for your transformative journey.

PEOPLE: THE CORE OF EVERY JOURNEY

At its core, redemptive recreation starts with the people. Who you invite on your journey is the most important decision you'll make. Whether it's family, friends, a faith community, or colleagues, the people are the ones who will shape the experience and create lasting memories.

I have had the privilege to work with a non-profit that plans redemptive experiences for non-profit leaders who are serving large organizations around the country. We begin by understanding the unique challenges this group faces. These leaders may be surrounded by people every day but often are lacking deep, restorative connections. A trip designed to help these leaders rest, restore, and reconnect with others statistically prevents burnout and fosters deeper relationships.

Another group I am working with is doing incredible work around the world. We ask *who* could benefit from a deeper connection with each other and a stronger understanding of this organization? Who are the people that are called to serve? Who would be an encouragement? Who needs encouragement?

If I am planning a trip with my son, I want to think about his point of view and what truly inspires him. If I have decided to go on a redemptive journey by myself, I take stock of what I need spiritually and emotionally and who I need as a mentor, guide, or partner.

Start with people.

Who are you inviting to share this experience? Who do you want to have a deeper relationship with this year? Who wants to be in a relationship with you and champion your journey with you?

You decide who.

PLACE: THE CATALYST FOR CHANGE

While people are at the heart of a redemptive journey, the *place* is the catalyst for transformation. The setting and the environment shape our experience, influences our emotions, and even changes how we view life and relationships. When we step out of our usual surroundings, we gain a new perspective.

Consider a snowmobiling trip in Alaska or a serene river adventure in Montana. These new environments create space for conversations that wouldn't happen in the familiar hustle of daily life. Something about being in a different place makes us more open, more reflective. It's why individuals and families seeking renewal may choose places like Moab, Utah, where the edge of a 1,500-foot cliff offers not just breathtaking views but a chance to reflect on life from a different angle.

If you are usually working in an office in Ohio, then spend a week in Santorini and see how your perspective shifts.

On our epic road trip adventure, we learned that our perspective changed each time we opened the door to a new place. Since the scenery was always changing, the family relationships became the constant in our lives. At one point, I took the family to Dallas to show them Dallas Theological Seminary, a place that was so incredibly transformative for me. In that case, I wasn't choosing a location that was unfamiliar to me, but rather one that I wanted to share with my children, a place that had a profound impact on their life and they had never even stepped foot on the campus. That was a place of significance for me because God taught me so much there. I wanted to introduce them to the professors and walk through the library. I wanted my children to see just a glimpse of the place and its impact on our lives, even if it was through the smile and tears on my face.

My wife's grandfather was born on the tiny Caribbean Island of Cayman Brac. Ever since our children were infants, we have taken them there and shared the history of the family and the islands through the eyes of their great-grandfather, the businesses he built, and the lives he touched. Now, when we bring friends to the island, our children know how to give the grand tour. They teach our friends how to scout for coconut sprouts and plant them so that they become a part of this special place. Our kids take them to the museum and point out important landmarks. They show them their favorite caves and snorkel spots. They know where to take the best pictures. The Cayman Islands, especially Cayman Brac, is special to us, and we invite others to experience it. It has changed us, and we love bringing people into the story of this place. We now even have a waterfront retreat to host you and your family! If you connect to a place, then you have a natural and redemptive way to connect with others as they experience that place for the first time with you!

Of course, planning a redemptive experience often involves exploring new terrain, but not always. Places change as seasons change, as people leave and move on. But here is the secret, as you start planning a trip or experience, just entering into that process with a different mindset is already changing you. Before you step foot in that airplane or turn on your vehicle, you have already begun the redemptive process in your mind. Renewing our minds needs to become a daily practice because it is where everything that we experience, everything that we do, starts and changes.

PROGRAM: THE AGENDA FOR THE SOUL

The *program* is where your intention comes into play. What will you do on this adventure? The program doesn't just refer to logistics or a schedule—it's about crafting an agenda, a vision even, that feeds your soul and brings you closer to the purpose of the journey.

We knew a few things as we set off on our RV trip. We knew we wanted to homeschool the kids. We wanted to work from the road. Those were the basics, but we had a bigger vision for the program. It was deeper than the logistics. We had a mission and vision that would outlast the days on the road.

Our mission was to experience all the natural, created world had to offer. We knew the National Parks were an easy place to start.

Our *vision* was that we and our children would forever appreciate nature and the wonder of Creation. Our *mission* was to create lasting memories through adventure and instill a sense of awe in their hearts for themselves, our family, and for others.

Vision is what we *see* and should scare us in a good way.

Mission is what we are going to do in response.

Our adventure was more than ticking locations off a list — and adding badges to our vest — it was about what we wanted for our souls. The program, then, involves hiking, exploring, and learning together. Every activity was designed to foster connection and growth toward a lifelong love of adventure! What we didn't realize was that we were creating LEGACY! Legacy are the things we put into motion today. One of our core values as a family is *adventure*. We communicate our value by saying we are "boundless in adventure." It conveys the idea of being limitless, fearless, and open to exploring new possibilities, experiences, and challenges. It suggests a mindset of curiosity, daring, and a willingness to push beyond boundaries. Now THAT is a program I can get behind, no matter what we do or where we go.

When considering your program, the investment of time and energy should yield a greater return than the sum of the events. Start with your vision and mission. For example, a road trip might seem like a simple logistical plan, but it can become an agenda for the soul if it's designed with intention. Time spent together, or alone, becomes time to communicate and explore values, create experiences, and capture memories that will shape the future.

The key to a good program is to ask good questions. *Will the time and energy invested produce something greater than the sum of its parts? Will the experiences yield a return that impacts not just the trip itself, but the lives of those involved long after they return home?*

Like any financial investment, consider the ROI. I would not invest my money in anything without expecting a higher return on investment. Is what you are investing in yielding a greater return? Am I going to know my children better? Are we going to draw closer as a family? Am I going to find answers to the questions I have in my life? Is what I am going to learn going to help others?

As you craft a program, ask yourself: How will each moment of your journey shape not just your adventure, but your legacy? Let every choice be an investment in deeper connection, personal growth, and the creation of memories that echo far beyond the trip itself.

PURSUIT: WHAT ARE YOU RUNNING TOWARD?

This is it. This is the *why* behind everything you do. Redemption is not a passive process—it is an active pursuit. You are redeeming your life in the pursuit of something greater, something worth the time you've been given. The question is, what is it?

At the "end" of our RV adventures, we found ourselves right back where we started. But something was different. The road we traveled hadn't just taken us to new places—it had taken us to a new understanding of ourselves and of God's presence in our journey. We realized that the destination was never the point. The pursuit itself had transformed us. Life on the road teaches you things you don't learn when standing still. You learn that home is not a place—it's found in the presence of God and the people He has placed in your life. That simplicity often leads to greater joy, and that letting go of excess—whether material or emotional—creates space for what truly matters. You learn to embrace the unexpected—the detours, the breakdowns, the unplanned stops—because sometimes, the greatest moments happen when things *don't* go according to your plan, but they always remain within God's plan. You learn patience when the journey takes longer than expected, and trust when you have to rely on His provision in unfamiliar places. You learn that gratitude grows in unexpected circumstances, and that some of the most beautiful moments come when you surrender control and simply follow where He leads. Most of all, you learn that life itself is a journey of faith, not just a pursuit of destinations. If you're only fixated on arriving somewhere — on reaching a goal, achieving success, or finding the perfect circumstances — you'll miss the beauty of the road God has placed you on right now. The journey changes you, just as it changed us. The miles we traveled weren't just measured in distance but in growth, in trust, in clarity, in the realization that what we were searching for wasn't a place at all — it was a deeper understanding of God's purpose for our lives.

So let me ask you a question:

What are you pursuing?

What do you truly want in life?

Not the surface-level answers, not what others expect of you, but deep down — what is your soul running toward? If you don't intentionally choose your pursuit, life will choose it for you. You will always be chasing something. The question is whether it will lead you toward redemption or leave you running in circles.

Here's what I know: Nothing changes until you decide to change. No transformation happens by accident. The moment you commit to pursuing a life of meaning, of purpose, of redemption, everything begins to shift. It won't happen overnight, and it won't always be easy, but it will be worth it.

When you have a clear mission and vision driven by your values, you create opportunities for transformation — not just for yourself, but for those around you. The right people will come together in the right place for a greater purpose. And in the end, it won't just be a collection of memories — it will be a redemptive journey. A reclaiming of time, purpose, and the life you were meant to live.

So, I ask you again: What are you running toward? Your pursuit will define your story. Make it one worth telling.

REDEMPTIVE REFLECTION
CHAPTER 8: DESIGNING POSSIBILITY

A redemptive journey isn't just about travel — it's about transformation. This reflection invites you to intentionally pursue change through people, place, program, and purpose. Use these prompts to shape your next meaningful experience and begin a journey that redefines how you live, love, and lead.

People — *Who is part of your redemptive story?*

___

Who are the people I want a deeper connection with this season?

___

108 | REDEMPTIVE PURSUITS

Place — *What environments stir something inside me?*

Program — *What is the soul-level vision for this experience?*

Purpose — *What value is driving this journey?*

What kind of legacy do I hope this pursuit will begin to build?

Pursuit — *What am I running toward?*

What kind of story do I want to tell about this pursuit — ten years from now?

Redemptive pursuits don't happen by accident — they begin with awareness, grow through intention, and thrive with courageous action. Whatever you're running toward, may it lead you deeper into purpose, connection, and life that truly matters.

CHAPTER 9

CONSECRATING TIME

*"How we spend our days is,
of course, how we spend our lives."*
ANNIE DILLARD

After planning and living these incredible redemptive experiences, the next logical question is "What now?" What happens when you return home? Now that you have experienced the mountaintop, how can you continue to see the other weeks of the year in a more redemptive light?

Think about it.

You saved the money. You adjusted your schedule. And then you went.

But life back home didn't just disappear or change magically. Most everything you left behind is still there. Do you really think you can go on a life-changing journey and then slip effortlessly back into the same ruts and routines? No way.

It is time to redefine what it means to come back from a transformative adventure. Traditionally, we treat vacations as sacred, set apart—those rare, precious weeks earned through hard work. Boarding a plane or packing a car carries the anticipation of something extraordinary. Those vacation weeks feel like a reward because of what we endured leading up to them.

But what if we flipped the script? What if those breathtaking moments weren't the exception, but the inspiration for a more intentional way of living the other weeks of the year? What if they weren't a reward, but a beginning?

LIVING LIGHT, LIVING FREE

What if we approached every week with the same sense of wonder and intentionality we usually reserve for a vacation? Imagine treating all fifty-two weeks as sacred, each one worthy of our best energy, focus, and care. Instead of elevating just a few weeks, we could infuse our entire year with purpose and meaning.

One of the most unexpected lessons we brought back from our time on the road was the simplicity and significance of gathering around a fire. Whether it was in a National Park, a campground, or a quiet spot in the middle of nowhere, the fire became the centerpiece of our evenings. It was where we slowed down, reflected on the day, and connected as a family without distractions.

But beyond just the fire itself, we learned something even more powerful: we didn't need as much as we thought we did — not just in terms of material possessions, but in the weight we carried in our hearts and minds. On the road, we lived light. Everything we packed had a purpose. Without the clutter of too many things, too many commitments, and too much noise, we found freedom — not just physically, but mentally and emotionally.

When we returned home, we realized the lessons from those fires didn't have to stay in the past. One evening, my son asked if he could build a fire in the fireplace. Without hesitation, he gathered the kindling and logs, stacked them just as he had learned on the road, and carefully struck a match. The process was second nature to him — something that had become deeply ingrained. Watching him, I realized how much those small, daily practices had shaped us.

As we sat by the fire that night, we talked about what we missed from our time adventuring. We realized it wasn't just the adventure—it was the clarity that came from stripping life down to what really mattered. When you live in an RV, you don't have space for excess, and you begin to understand how little you need to be happy. Back at home, surrounded by far more than we needed, it became clear that much of it wasn't necessary. The simplicity we experienced wasn't just about physical space; it was about how we spent our time, how we prioritized what mattered, and how much lighter life felt when we let go of the things weighing us down.

That moment in front of the fire led us to make real changes. We started letting go of things we didn't need. We created more intentional spaces. We made time for what mattered most. We even brought back the tradition of "fire nights"—regular evenings spent gathering, talking about life, and keeping that same spirit of connection alive.

The biggest shift was realizing that we didn't have to wait for a vacation or a road trip to live with purpose and intention. The lessons we learned around those campfires didn't belong only to the wilderness; they belonged at home, too. We had spent so much of our lives chasing the next big thing, believing the most meaningful moments happened somewhere else. But purpose and meaning aren't reserved for rare adventures.

They are a way of life, a way of thinking and being that can shape every single day.

When we approach life with this mindset, the entire year becomes an opportunity to experience purposeful moments. Elevating every regular day means investing in a life we don't need to escape from—a life that celebrates what God is doing each day. Each morning becomes a redemptive pursuit, an opportunity to set out on a mission, not just hit reset.

By reframing vacations this way, those precious days become a leveling-up opportunity for intentional recalibration. Each time we take a restorative break, we're given a chance to realign—to re-center our gifts and reflect on our purpose—so that upon our return, we're energized to pursue life in a new way.

This is what it means to redeem your time. Every day comes with a renewed perspective. We stop spending the year waiting for a break. Instead, we start living for a purpose—running toward, not away from, our true calling.

REFRAME AS YOU RETURN

Another practical way to think about this is to spend time reframing before you return. While you were away, you removed the constraints and gained new perspectives. Rather than allowing yourself to drift back into old routines, set your intention before leaving the redemptive trip. It can be as simple as writing a one-line objective statement for your return.

But it must go deeper than writing words on paper.

I see it all the time when people attend a conference or retreat and create a powerful mission statement. What happens next? They frame it, hang it on a wall—and go right back to living the same way they always have. Your goal is not just to hang a mission statement; your goal is to live it. It should be seen and felt in everything you do.

Gary Vaynerchuk said, "Please think about your legacy because you are writing it every day." Living redemptively when you return home is infinitely more valuable than just writing about it.

The essence of pursuing something requires action. You are returning home to actively pursue what you connected to when you were fully alive and honest with yourself. When you left home, you were on one path; but now, you have chosen a different one. You are returning with a framework for thinking about time differently. The questions you worked through to plan this redemptive trip can now be applied to any week, month, or year.

For every category of your life — your job, marriage, friendships, hobbies, community, even politics — you can run your pursuits through a clearer lens to determine how you want to pursue a more meaningful experience.

All pursuits can be reframed.

All time can be redeemed.

To turn the things we are chasing into more redemptive pursuits, imagine pouring all your goals, dreams, and efforts through a "funnel" that guides your focus, followed by a "filter" that aligns with your deeper values. This approach creates clarity about what's worth pursuing and helps reveal what might just be a fleeting ambition.

THE FUNNEL

Start by pouring everything into three foundational elements:

1. **People:** Who is this for? Who am I serving or impacting? This could include your family, your community, or even a larger audience.

2. **Place:** Where am I rooted? Where does this pursuit take place? It might mean a physical location, a social environment, or a platform you're building.

Is my environment adding or taking away from my ability to grow and thrive?

3. **Program**: What am I creating? This is your unique expression or project. Think of this as your blueprint — something that, over time, evolves and grows.

Once your pursuits flow through these categories, ask yourself honestly about each one:

What is the real purpose? Is it to provide for others? To build a platform? To make a lot of money? Or perhaps it's simply to create something beautiful or impactful. Brutal honesty here is critical for seeing where your pursuits genuinely align with a redemptive purpose.

THE FILTER

Before moving forward, filter every decision through a lens that reflects your mission, vision, values.

1. What is your personal mission, and do your plans align with it?

2. Consider your long-term vision for your life, work, and family — does your current schedule bring you closer to that picture?

3. Reflect on your core values. Core values are the fundamental beliefs that guide your actions and decisions. They act as a personal compass, helping you stay true to your mission and vision throughout the process. When you clearly define your core values, you create a solid foundation for all your choices, ensuring that every step you take is in alignment with what truly matters to you.

4. Clarify your purpose: what drives you at your very core?

5. Evaluate your pursuits: are the actions you take truly advancing that purpose? This comprehensive filter ensures that every choice not only brings personal gain but also contributes to something larger.

I once chased after things blindly until I learned to listen for the early alarm bells and adjust my course. I invite you to do the same, aligning your decisions with what truly matters so you can shape a life that resonates from the inside out. This process is the standard against which all pursuits are evaluated. It helps ensure that what you pour through the funnel isn't just about personal gain but contributes to something larger, bringing redemptive value to both you and those around you.

The goal is to reshape your life from the inside out, from the truest part of yourself, rather from the outside in, from what your schedule is demanding of you. There was a time when I pursued a goal so relentlessly that I ignored all the warning signs. After stepping back and facing some hard truths about my life, I learned to build a healthier, more balanced existence. Now, I notice those red flags early and can adjust my course before things go off track.

Your life is too important to not do this. Your time on this earth is too short to wait.

CEASE THE STRIVING

Ironically, I'm not here to urge you to set lofty goals or push yourself harder. The beauty of this journey lies in its paradox: it's an invitation to let go of the grind and embrace the art of living fully.

As you truly connect to your unique calling, you will find incredible peace in saying, "No" and in doing less. The overscheduled life is likely an unexamined life. As you step back and examine, you can make choices that more closely align to your highest purpose.

It's not intuitive. We've been conditioned to think more is better. We are naturally meant to create, contribute, and grow, yet we are often conditioned to pursue outcomes that leave us unfulfilled.

When you are clear about your purpose, you can remove the things that are hindering you and start to enjoy your life again because of the peace that will be present. When I was growing up, we spent hours playing in the woods behind my house. I used to think of this "play time" as wasted time, but now I have learned that it's in this playful exploration that I can heal. In this setting, I find clarity each day to be present to the pursuits God is really calling me toward and leave behind my ego that pushes me to do more to impress others.

Everything you need to know—all the answers you are searching for—are on the other side of your ego. Redemptive recreation, whether for an extended period of time or during a short walk in the woods, quiets the ego and keeps you focused on your true north.

When you come home, stay connected to that true part of yourself that knows the difference between useless striving for the ego and redemptive pursuits that are part of your calling.

REDEMPTIVE REFLECTION
CHAPTER 9: RECLAIMING THE SACRED

Returning home from a transformative experience is not the end—it's the beginning. This reflection will help you shift from treating vacations as an escape to seeing all of life as sacred ground—where time, space, and pursuit are consecrated with meaning and purpose.

What daily or weekly rhythms can help me carry the peace, clarity, and joy from my redemptive experiences into my everyday life?

What clutter needs to go?

What would it look like to live light, live free, and focus only on what truly matters?

What do I need to run towards instead of from?

What filter — mission, vision, values — can help me shape better decisions with my time?

REDEMPTIVE PURSUITS

Is there a space or ritual — like a fire night, walk in nature, or moment of reflection — that brings me back to what matters?

How can I turn sacred moments into sacred rhythms?

You don't need another vacation to live fully. You need a way to carry the clarity home.

Consecrate your time. Filter your pursuits. Reframe your return. This is how you live redemptively—not just on the mountaintop, but in the everyday moments that shape your life.

CHAPTER 10

THE ROAD TO REDEMPTION

*"There are far, far better things ahead
than any we leave behind."*

C.S. LEWIS

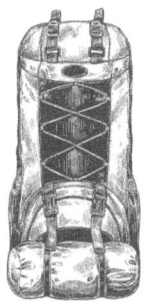

When Polly and I set out on this journey, we thought we knew what we were searching for. We imagined ourselves moving to a new city, a new state—maybe even another country. We pictured ourselves immersed in new cultures, standing at the edge of the world, chasing the horizon, and filling our days with excitement. In our dreams, we were adventurers, and we believed that if we could just find the right place, the right experience, or the right moment, everything would change.

But as the days turned into weeks and the miles stretched behind us, we began to realize something profound: the change we were seeking wasn't just about where we were going—it was about who we were becoming. The adventures we thought we were chasing became a catalyst for something much deeper. With every new experience, every unfamiliar place, and every challenge, our perspectives began to shift. What started as an outward search turned into an inward transformation. In pursuing the unknown, we uncovered new passions, new dreams, and—most importantly—a way of being we hadn't known was possible.

It turns out the greatest adventure wasn't waiting for us in some faraway place. It was within us, waiting to be discovered. And the same thing is waiting for you. The Ralph Waldo Emerson phrase, "Life is a journey, not a destination" is truer today than when it was first uttered simply because we have so much information at our fingertips to actually see life unfold before our eyes and be captured in so many different ways.

THE REDEMPTION OF PERSPECTIVE

When we launched on our journey, we thought we needed an escape. A reset. A fresh start. But what we needed was redemption—the redemption of our time, our priorities, our way of thinking, our souls, our story. As we embarked on the process of resetting and reframing, something extraordinary happened. Our family began to craft a completely new vision for what truly mattered. What began as a restless pursuit of adventure turned into the rediscovery of purpose. We saw our values more clearly than ever before. We thought we had been setting off in search of excitement and discovery, but what we found was something far more profound: a deeper understanding of what we were truly chasing—and why.

We left looking for adventure but returned with clarity. We left seeking change but returned with a renewed sense of mission and purpose. We left wanting to experience something new but came back with a transformed way of living that will guide us for the rest of our lives.

THE JOURNEY AHEAD

Perhaps you've found yourself asking the same questions we once did:

- "Let's just move to another country."
- "We need a sabbatical."
- "Should we take the kids out of school and do something different?"

If these thoughts have ever crossed your mind, let me encourage you—this is the beginning of something incredible.

Maybe it is time for a change of scenery. Maybe you should get away for a while. See the world. Experience something new.

But know this: the real discovery won't just come from where you go, but from what you learn along the way.

You may set out thinking you need a change in place, but what you may truly need is a change in perspective. You may believe you are running toward something, but it's just as important to understand what you might be running from. Sometimes, the only way to see your life clearly is to step away from it for a little while. And as you do, you'll begin to notice what needs to slow down and what needs to speed up. You'll start to uncover the things that have been holding you back. And in that space—between the leaving and the returning—renewal begins. The restoration of your mind. The redemption of your soul. Because the greatest discovery of all—the one that transcends every place and every time—isn't found in a destination. It's found in learning how to truly live.

A LIFE WORTH REDEEMING

This is not about curating an Instagram-perfect life. It's not about collecting beautiful moments just for the sake of having them. This is about becoming a more authentic human being.

Our travels did not just give us stories to tell; they reshaped the way we live each day. They taught us how to redeem our time—not just for the sake of adventure, but for the sake of living better in the ordinary moments. The big adventures taught us how to craft better, richer, more meaningful adventures in our daily lives.

So, where do you go from here?

Maybe the better question is: Who will you become from here?

This is an invitation. Not just to travel, but to reimagine your life. To redeem the time you've been given. To stop waiting for the perfect moment and start taking the steps toward a life that is truly yours.

And as you step forward, know this—God loves you more than you can fathom. His plans for you are greater than anything you could dream for yourself. You are not alone in this journey. His hand is guiding you, His grace is sustaining you, and His love is calling you to more.

I believe in you, but even more than that, God believes in you. He created you with purpose, with gifts the world needs, and with a story that is still unfolding. No mistake, no delay, no detour is too great for Him to redeem.

So go, not just toward a new destination, but toward the abundant life He has for you. Trust Him. Walk boldly. And never forget—you are deeply, endlessly, and perfectly loved. The greatest journey of your life isn't just about discovery—it's about the redemptive pursuit of reclaiming what truly matters, embracing your purpose, and stepping into the life you were meant to live.

REDEMPTIVE REFLECTION
CHAPTER 10: THE WAY FORWARD

Redemption isn't a destination — it's a journey. As you reflect on where you've been and where you're going, this final chapter invites you to embrace what's been transformed in you and imagine what's still to come.

What do I hope to discover along the way — about myself, my values, or my purpose?

_____

_____

_____

_____

How can I bring redemptive intention into the everyday moments that lie ahead?

_____

_____

_____

What does it mean to live fully — right where I am?

Who do I want to become?

What parts of my life are worth redeeming now?

What is God inviting me into next?

You don't have to go far to live fully. You just have to follow the road that leads home — to yourself, to God, to what matters most. This is your redemptive pursuit. And the best is still ahead.

> **THIS MAY BE THE END OF THE BOOK, BUT HOPEFULLY THIS IS THE START OF SOMETHING NEW FOR YOU.**

If something stirred in you—don't let it fade.

This is your invitation to take the next step.

Because let's be honest…

You've built strategies for your business.

You've invested in your work, your success, your ambitions.

But when it comes to your life—and your legacy—have you ever truly defined what matters and clearly defined it?

If someone asked what you or your family stand for… could you answer?

Most people can't.

We drift. We hustle. We react.

We confuse motion for meaning and wonder why it still feels off.

But the people you love deserve more than that.

And so do you.

Go to
WWW.REDEMPTIVEPURSUITS.COM/BOOK

Explore practical tools, stories, and next steps to help you live—and lead—with clarity, conviction, and purpose.

This isn't about being perfect.

It's about being intentional.

It's about designing your life the same way you'd design a great company:

- *With values.*
- *With vision.*
- *With a mission that matters.*

You are not just closing a book.

You're opening the door to a new way of living.

DISCOVER WHAT MATTERS.

LIVE LIKE IT DOES.

ABOUT THE AUTHOR

Kenny Klepacki is a husband, father, pilot, adventurer, and entrepreneur who married into a successful multi-generational family—and discovered firsthand what it means to live with purpose and build a life that matters.

A storyteller at heart and strategist by trade, Kenny has helped build businesses, advise large family enterprises, and guide high-capacity individuals toward a deeper kind of success—one rooted in vision, mission, values, and legacy. But behind every venture is one heartbeat: *to help people discover what matters and to live like it does.*

Redemptive Pursuits is his trail journal—born from both personal triumphs and trials—and an invitation to those who feel the quiet pull toward something more significant.

Kenny lives between coastal Florida and the Cayman Islands with his wife and children, where he continues to chase adventure, clarity, and calling—with his eyes on eternity and his feet in the present.

www.ingramcontent.com/pod-product-compliance
Lightning Source LLC
Chambersburg PA
CBHW020938090426
42736CB00010B/1185